Searchlight
BOOKS™

What Can
We Do about
Pollution?

How Can We Reduce

Nuclear Pollution?

Samantha S. Bell

Lerner Publications ◆ Minneapolis

Content Consultant: Mark Embrechts, Professor of Nuclear Engineering, Rensselaer Polytechnic Institute

Lerner Publications Company
A division of Lerner Publishing Group, Inc.
241 First Avenue North
Minneapolis, MN 55401 USA

For reading levels and more information, look up this title at
www.lernerbooks.com.

Library of Congress Cataloging-in-Publication Data

Bell, Samantha, author.
  How can we reduce nuclear pollution? / by Samantha S. Bell.
    pages cm — (Searchlight books. What can we do about pollution?)
  Audience: Age: 8-11.
  Audience: Grades 4-6.
  Includes bibliographical references and index.
  ISBN 978-1-4677-9516-6 (lb : alk. paper) — ISBN 978-1-4677-9705-4 (pb : alk. paper) — ISBN 978-1-4677-9706-1 (eb pdf)
  1. Radioactive pollution—Juvenile literature. 2. Radioactive waste disposal—Juvenile literature. I. Title.
  TD196.R3B45 2016
  621.48'38—dc23
                      2015027077

Manufactured in the United States of America
1 – VP – 12/31/15

Contents

Chapter 1

NUCLEAR POLLUTION

Nuclear pollution is the waste produced when nuclear energy is created. But what is nuclear energy? And how is it different from other forms of energy?

Nuclear reactions can help scientists create electricity. What metal does a nuclear reaction start with?

Nuclear energy provides electricity to millions of people. It is created through nuclear reactions. Nuclear reactions start with a radioactive metal called uranium. Radioactive substances give off radiation, a dangerous and powerful form of energy.

URANIUM IS A FAIRLY COMMON ELEMENT. THERE IS ABOUT FORTY TIMES MORE URANIUM THAN SILVER IN THE WORLD.

Uranium is mined from the ground. Like other metals, uranium is made up of tiny particles called atoms. Atoms are so small we cannot even see them. But scientists have a way to split them. Splitting atoms is called fission. When the atoms are split, a nuclear reaction occurs.

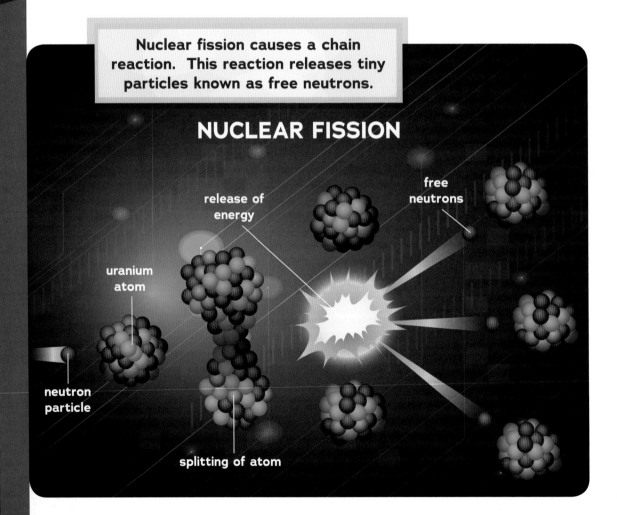

Nuclear fission causes a chain reaction. This reaction releases tiny particles known as free neutrons.

NUCLEAR FISSION

free
neutrons

release of
energy

uranium
atom

neutron
particle

splitting of atom

The atoms release energy. This energy can be used to boil water. The boiling water makes steam. And the steam powers a machine called a turbine. The turbine helps create electricity.

Workers repair a turbine at a nuclear plant in Japan.

In France, about 75 percent of electricity comes from nuclear energy. About 20 percent of the electricity used in the United States is made from nuclear energy.

Nuclear energy is called clean-air energy. Unlike energy from coal, oil, and natural gas, nuclear energy does not create air pollution. It does not cause global warming. But it can result in other kinds of dangerous pollution.

For example, some pollution is created when uranium is mined. Water pollution occurs when the uranium is used as fuel. And the used uranium produces highly radioactive waste. If the radioactive waste pollutes the environment, it can make people very sick. It can also harm wildlife and their habitats. Let's find out what we can do to reduce the effects of nuclear pollution!

Workers wear protective suits when they are dealing with radioactive materials.

Chapter 2

MINING POLLUTION

Scientists need uranium to make nuclear energy. Uranium is found almost everywhere in the earth's crust. Some areas have a lot of uranium. But getting uranium out of the ground and ready to use can cause pollution.

Some uranium is mined from open pits. Why do scientists need uranium?

Workers get the uranium by mining it. If the uranium is near the surface, workers might use strip mining. In strip mining, workers dig huge, open pits deep into the rock. Large trucks haul chunks of mixed rock and uranium, called ore, out of the pits.

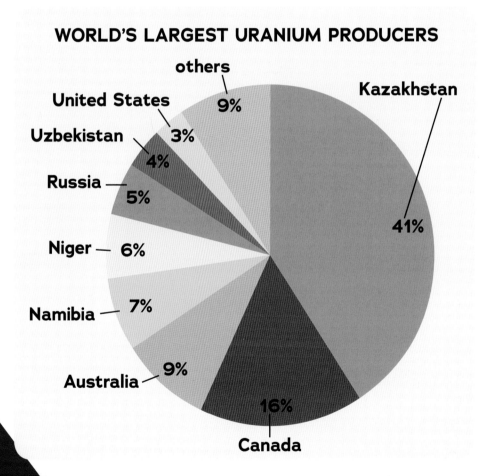

WORLD'S LARGEST URANIUM PRODUCERS

others

United States

Uzbekistan

Russia

Niger — 6%

Namibia — 7%

Australia — 9%

9%

3%

4%

5%

Kazakhstan

41%

16%

Canada

If the uranium is too far down for an open pit, workers can use underground mining. They use long drills to cut into the rock and ore. This creates shafts and tunnels. Then the ore is blasted into pieces. Sometimes elevators in the shafts bring the small pieces back to the surface. Other times trucks carry the ore out of the mines.

In both strip mining and underground mining, the ore is taken to a mill and crushed. A chemical is then added to the ore. This process separates the uranium from the rest of the rock. The tiny pieces of rock and other minerals left behind are called tailings.

This mill uses large tanks of chemicals to remove uranium from ore.

Effects of Mining Pollution

Mining uranium can harm people and the environment. Strip mining leaves huge pits and large piles of tailings. Over time, the tailings decay. They produce radioactive by-products including harmful radon gas. People who work in the mines can breathe in the by-products and become very sick.

This old uranium mill is covered so that radioactive by-products do not escape from the remaining tailings.

Many people get their drinking water from open reservoirs like this one. If radioactive materials get into this water, people who drink it could develop cancer.

Wind and water might also move the radioactive materials from the tailings. Sometimes those materials get into sources of drinking water. People who drink it can become very sick.

A Geiger counter is a device that uses an electric current to detect and measure radiation of all types.

Solutions to Mining Pollution

Many people are working hard to limit the harmful waste from mining. Older mining sites are being cleaned up and covered. Piles of tailings are being moved away from homes to safer areas. Scientists also check the soil around mines to make sure it is safe. They use Geiger counters to check radiation levels.

Some uranium is now mined using in-situ leaching (ISL). *In situ* means "in place," and *leaching* means "dissolving out." In this type of mining, a solution with water and extra oxygen is pushed deep into the ground and into the uranium ore. The uranium dissolves into the water and is pumped to the surface. ISL does not create tailings and causes much less radiation.

In-situ leaching equipment removes uranium from a field in Nebraska. The process is less harmful to the environment than strip mining.

Chapter 3

WATER POLLUTION

Like other types of power plants, nuclear plants use steam to create electricity. Steam is made from heated water. So, nuclear plants need large amounts of water to create the steam.

Nuclear plants create lots of steam. Where do these plants get their water?

Power plants get water from nearby lakes, rivers, or oceans. As the water is used, salts can build up in it. So can heavy metals such as copper and zinc. Some of this polluted water may be sent back into the environment.

THIS NUCLEAR PLANT USES WATER FROM A NEARBY RIVER.

Just as a swimming pool cools you on a hot day, this huge tank of water cools the used fuel rods.

Nuclear plants need water for other reasons too. Before uranium can be used, it is made into small pellets. The pellets are placed into metal tubes to make fuel rods. When the atoms are split, they create a lot of heat. The fuel rods become very hot. Nuclear power plants use huge tanks of water to help cool the rods. It takes about ten years to cool the rods. As the rods cool, the water warms. Sometimes the heated water goes back into the lakes, rivers, and oceans.

What Effects Does Water Pollution Have?

Polluted water harms fish and other animals that live in the area. Salts and heavy metals in the water can be toxic, or poisonous. If the water is too warm, some kinds of wildlife cannot live in it. Some species may migrate away. Sometimes plants and animals die off.

New York's Indian Point Energy Center releases a lot of heated water. Scientists believe that millions of fish die there each year as a result.

Fish that can live in the warmer water are in danger too. If a power plant shuts down for maintenance, the water will become cooler. The sudden change in temperature often kills thousands of fish and fish eggs at one time.

MANY ANIMALS RELY ON FISH FOR FOOD. SO WHEN LARGE NUMBERS OF FISH DIE, OTHER ANIMALS ARE AFFECTED TOO.

These large, gray tanks are part of the water-cleaning system at a new nuclear power plant.

What Are the Solutions to Water Pollution?

There are ways to protect the water. Filters in nuclear plants help make the water clean again. The filters remove some of the salts, heavy metals, and radioactive particles. People who live nearby can also use small filters in their homes to make water safer to drink.

Thanks to EPA guidelines, many lakes and rivers near nuclear plants have healthy numbers of fish.

In 1972, the US Congress passed a law called the Clean Water Act. Under this law, the Environmental Protection Agency (EPA) makes the rules about cooling systems in nuclear plants. The EPA also helps decide what the temperature of the returned water should be.

New cooling systems are also designed with wildlife in mind. State agencies meet with nuclear plant operators. They work together to find the best cooling systems for the fish and other animals in the area.

A worker helps construct a new cooling tower at a nuclear plant in Tennessee.

Chapter 4

HIGH-LEVEL WASTE

Every eighteen to twenty-four months, used fuel rods must be removed from a nuclear power plant. They are now radioactive waste, also called high-level waste. But there is no permanent place in the United States to store this waste. For now, the spent fuel is stored at the nuclear plants in steel and concrete containers.

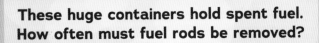

These huge containers hold spent fuel. How often must fuel rods be removed?

Sometimes the rods are not moved or stored correctly. When spent fuel is not handled properly, radioactive waste goes into the environment. In rare cases, an accident may occur at a nuclear power plant.

This robot was designed to look for radioactive fuel rods after an accident. People can operate the robot from a safe distance.

After the Chernobyl disaster, workers built a large structure to cover the damaged reactor. This structure limited the amount of radiation that entered the environment.

Effects of High-Level Waste

In 1986, there was an explosion in the nuclear power plant in Chernobyl, Ukraine. In 2011, a tsunami disabled the power supply and cooling system of three nuclear reactors in Fukushima, Japan. These accidents leaked high-level waste into the areas nearby. This waste can seriously harm people and animals. Its radiation can cause burns, sickness, cancer, and even death.

When accidents occur at nuclear power plants, people must leave their homes to escape the radiation. In Chernobyl, thirty people died within ninety days of the accident. The first month after the accident, 116,000 people were evacuated. In the years following, 220,000 more people had to move. The accident in Fukushima forced more than 100,000 people to leave their homes. Many of these people were still unable to return five years later.

A worker tests a Japanese man for radiation after the Fukushima disaster in 2011.

Solutions to High-Level Waste

Because radioactive waste is so dangerous, it must be stored where it cannot hurt anyone. Some scientists believe we should put the spent fuel in storage areas deep in the earth. They think this would be the safest place to keep it. Other scientists believe this may not be the best place for radioactive waste. After all, accidents can happen underground too. In New Mexico in 2014, an underground container with nuclear waste burst open. It sent radiation up through a shaft and into the environment.

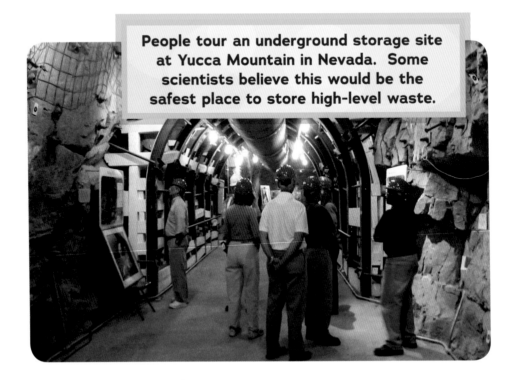

People tour an underground storage site at Yucca Mountain in Nevada. Some scientists believe this would be the safest place to store high-level waste.

A truck carries high-level waste to a storage facility.

Scientists are still working on a permanent solution. For now, we must rely on the rules that government agencies make. The Department of Energy plans ways to handle the waste safely. The Department of Transportation decides how the waste should be moved. The Nuclear Regulatory Commission controls where the waste will be stored. Strict rules help keep people, animals, and the environment safe.

A scientist holds a container full of thorium pellets. Thorium can also be used to make nuclear energy.

Also, a few nuclear plants use a different type of fuel. Instead of uranium, they use a material called thorium. This fuel is more expensive to make. But it creates much less radioactive waste.

Chapter 5

FOR THE FUTURE

Many kinds of power plants generate electricity. Power plants that use coal, oil, or natural gas create huge amounts of pollution. Other types of energy are very clean. This includes electricity created from sunlight and wind. But these sources do not yet create nearly enough power to meet people's needs.

Coal plants put tons of pollution into the air. What problems do other electricity sources have?

Nuclear power plants do not cause global warming. That is why many scientists believe nuclear energy is the best choice for the environment. Other scientists are worried about the possible dangers of nuclear pollution. When nuclear waste gets into the environment, it can cause great harm. But if all the safety rules are followed, accidents at nuclear power plants are extremely rare.

The steam from a nuclear plant does not harm the environment.

One of the best ways to help stop nuclear pollution is to learn about it. You can find information about nuclear waste at the library or online. Research where the uranium mines are located. Find out what kinds of mines they are. Also, find out whether the areas around them have been cleaned up. Locate nuclear power plants as well. Learn about the water near the plants and how the wildlife is doing.

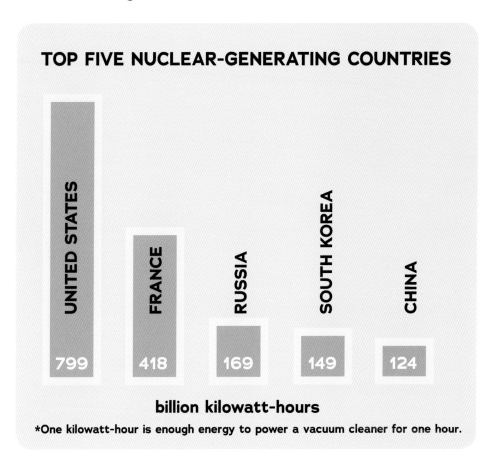

TOP FIVE NUCLEAR-GENERATING COUNTRIES

UNITED STATES — 799
FRANCE — 418
RUSSIA — 169
SOUTH KOREA — 149
CHINA — 124

billion kilowatt-hours
*One kilowatt-hour is enough energy to power a vacuum cleaner for one hour.

YOUR LETTER COULD HELP CONVINCE
LEADERS TO MAKE BETTER LAWS.

When you have information, you can write letters or
e-mails to your representatives in the government. Ask
them to pass laws to clean up the mining areas. Tell
them your concerns about water temperature and its
effects on fish. Encourage them to help find a way to
store high-level waste.

It is also a good idea to learn about other energy sources. What kinds of pollution do these sources cause? Compare them with nuclear pollution. Write about your ideas or concerns in your letter. Let your government leaders know what you think about nuclear energy. Together, we can work toward a world free of nuclear pollution!

Solar and wind power are very clean. But they are typically more expensive than other types of electricity.

Glossary

crust: the outer part of the earth

decay: to break down or rot

dissolve: to mix with a liquid so the resulting liquid is the same throughout

Geiger counter: an instrument for detecting radioactive substances

global warming: a warming of Earth's atmosphere and oceans, caused by an increase in air pollution

ore: a rock that contains a certain substance, such as uranium

radioactive: giving off rays of energy or particles caused by the breaking apart of atoms

shaft: an opening or passage that goes straight down

tsunami: a huge sea wave created by an earthquake or volcanic eruption

turbine: an engine fitted with a series of blades spun around by the pressure of steam or water

waste: material left over or thrown away

wildlife: nonhuman living things, especially animals in their natural environment

Learn More about Nuclear Pollution

Books

Benoit, Peter. *Nuclear Meltdowns*. New York: Scholastic, 2013. Benoit gives readers a look at nuclear disasters throughout history.

Doeden, Matt. *Finding Out about Nuclear Energy*. Minneapolis: Lerner, 2014. This book contains colorful photos and lots of interesting facts about nuclear energy.

Owen, Ruth. *Energy from Atoms: Nuclear Power*. New York: PowerKids Press, 2013. Owen explores how scientists are able to create electricity using nuclear power.

Websites

Kid's Korner: Nuclear Power
http://www.fplsafetyworld.com/?ver=kkblue&utilid=fplforkids&id=16182
Visit this site for a closer look at how fission works.

US Energy Information Administration: Energy Kids
http://www.eia.gov/kids/energy.cfm?page=nuclear_home-basics
This website is packed with fascinating information on how nuclear energy works.

US Environmental Protection Agency: Nuclear Power Plants
http://www.epa.gov/rpdweb01/nuclear-power-plants.html
Learn about nuclear power plants on the EPA's informative website.

Index

Photo Acknowledgments

The images in this book are used with the permission of: © Tomas Sereda/iStockphoto, p. 4;
© MarcelC/iStockphoto, p. 5; © BlueRingMedia/Shutterstock Images, p. 6; © Kiyoshi Ota/
Bloomberg/Getty Images, p. 7; © Andrey Krav/iStockphoto, p. 8; © ChiccoDodiFC/Shutterstock
Images, p. 9; © Inge Gajczak/iStockphoto, p. 10; © Red Line Editorial, pp. 11, 35; © Pavel Kosek/
Shutterstock Images, p. 12; © Energy Fuels Resources (USA) Inc., p. 13; © Department of Energy/
Nuclear Regulatory Commission, pp. 14, 31; © kokleong/iStockphoto, p. 15; © zlikovec/Shutterstock
Images, p. 16; © Nuclear Regulatory Commission, pp. 17, 20, 30; © hornyak/Shutterstock Images,
p. 18; © Michael Utech/iStockphoto, p. 19; © Tony Fischer CC2.0, p. 21; © overcrew/iStockphoto,
p. 22; © Georgia Power Company, p. 23; © Mark Zaleski/AP Images, pp. 24, 25; © US National
Nuclear Security Administration, p. 26; © Kyodo/AP Images, p. 27; © tinta/Shutterstock Images,
p. 28; © Wally Santana/AP Images, p. 29; © Pallava Bagla/Corbis, p. 32; © titop81/iStockphoto,
p. 33; © Martin Lisner/iStockphoto, p. 34; © Sirikornt/iStockphoto, p. 36; © Gong Hangxu/
iStockphoto, p. 37.

Front Cover: © Vlaclav Volrab/Shutterstock Images.

Main body text set in Adrianna Regular 14/20.
Typeface provided by Chank.